God Looked Beyond

My Faults

And Saw My Needs

Linda Davis

THREE SKILLET

GOD LOOKED BEYOND MY FAULTS AND SAW MY NEEDS,
Davis, Linda

First Edition

Title by Minister Rhonda McDuffie

◐♥◐ THREE SKILLET

www.ThreeSkilletPublishing.com

Cover and Author Photo by Farley L. Dunn

ISBN: 978-1-943189-27-4

Dedication

I dedicate this book to my dear friend, Ann, who won me to the Lord, and my dear mother, who was there for me, and lastly, to the God of my life.

Introduction

This book is about the mistakes I made without counting the cost. How I was out in the world, until I had got in a place where I needed God and wanted Him to help me but did not want to get saved. My life was out of control. I got possessed by bad demon spirits. The demons would torment me in bad ways. I was not serious with God until this point. I finally got serious with God and got delivered and filled with the Holy Spirit. How I became happy and on fire for God at the age of 45 years old, and

God called me to go out and minister to people. That is what I am doing and I am happy. I finally found peace in God. God loves me so much and He put up with my faults until I changed my life for the better. He saw in me what I did not. He saw what I could become. Praise God, and to God be the glory! Hallelujah!

God Looked Beyond
My Faults
And Saw My Needs

I WAS born to Mose and Violet Stepp on January 7, 1943. My family lived in a little town called Ormondsville, N.C. I had one brother, Freeman Ray Stepp, who was three and a half years older than me. He was the only sibling I ever had.

My granddaddy was also from Ormondsville. My mother's parents were Lawerence and Maybelle Bowen. My maternal granddaddy and grandmother moved to Dudley, N.C.

When my granddaddy lost his third wife, he advertised in the Goldsboro newspaper for a new wife. He met Miss Lucille for the first time when he was 88. She was a lovely woman, and we all loved her so much. Papa (as we knew him) died a happy man at 93 years of age.

When I was about four or five years old, we moved to Dudley also. We moved into a house, but we had no electricity, no running water, and no bathroom. We had no car, so my daddy would walk to nearby Goldsboro to work. My daddy drank beer frequently, but he worked and took care of his family. Times were bad back then and we were very poor.

My daddy had no education, and my mother was a housewife, as women often were then. My daddy quit school in the third grade. His father passed away when he was thirteen years old. He and his brothers had to work to take care of their family. His brothers were named John and Raymond. His sisters were Annie, Laura, Lucy, and Bet.

Around the time we moved to Dudley was the time I started school. My brother and I started our new school at Brogden School, near where we lived in Dudley.

My daddy went to Virginia to purchase a car. We waited for him to come home with our first car. I remember taking baths in tin tubs. We had a few toys, but we played outside mostly. My brother was usually off somewhere by himself playing, so I learned to play by myself.

Eventually, we got electricity. My mother would pump water for the washing machine; it was the old ringer-style washing machine. When it was almost time for Santa to come, I would always wash up all of my toys so he would see how well taken care of they were.

Later, we got the chance to move less than a mile away. At this house we had lights, running water, and a bathroom. Thank God! We lived on a farm there. We had 15 acres of tobacco, a garden with corn, a cow, two goats, and a few pigs and chickens.

My brother and I would get up early before school to help out on the farm. It was hard work. We were poor and did not have the right equipment so we did the best we could. We had a mule and a wagon to bring the tobacco out of the field to the tobacco barn. That was where we put it on the sticks and put it in the barn to cure. We had lots of people to help us. My cousin, Charles, and I would stay with our grand-parents. My Aunt Dollie would take care of us a lot.

I had nine boy cousins, and I was the only girl for the longest time. None of the boys would play with me except Jimmy. He would play paper dolls and other things with me.

My Aunt Dollie was my mother's sister. My mother had two sisters, Dollie and Edith. She had five brothers, Thelbert, Earl, Thad, CL, and Chester. They were all beautiful men and women. My granddaddy once told me he never lost any sleep over them because of them doing wrong things.

We met a new family not too far from us. Mr. Watis and Mrs. Edna were their names. They had three children, Gene, Connie, and Tony. We still didn't have any TV at this time so we would go to their house to watch TV.

People back then would turn off the lights to watch TV. Mr. Watis started asking me to sit in his lap, so I did. That is when he started playing with my private parts. I never told anyone until much later in my life, and then, only my mother. They would have birthday parties and other gatherings, and we always went because we were too poor to have a party.

We would go to the coast fishing a lot. We had a lot of fun doing that.

WE WERE still farming and I met a man who asked me would I like to keep his horses. So I did. I would ride, ride, ride those horses all of the time. I sometimes would ride them bareback or without a bridle. That is where I learned to love horses. I had them for years after I was grown.

We went to town every Saturday. My

daddy would give us money and we would all go our separate ways. There were three movie theaters in town, and I would hit two of them. Then I would go get something to eat and then go back to meet up with my parents to return home. People weren't as mean back then as they are now. People weren't afraid to let their children out of their sight.

We got two goats, Brownie and Piggy. We milked them and drank their milk. They both had babies at the same time. I played with them like they were my babies. I named them Tom and Jerry, after the cartoon, of course. My daddy eventually got rid of them. I can't remember why. I was so sad. We had hog killings and our neighbors would help us. Finally, the man came back for his horses. I was so sad.

We had lots of woods back behind our house. I spent a lot of time in them. There were really high hills back deep in the woods, and that is where I went to play. I would hang on the vines and swing down the hills. I had lots of fun.

We would go to Greene County a lot. My daddy's family lived there. My Aunt Lucy took care of me some when I was young. She was very special to me. My Granddaddy Stepp died at an early age when my daddy was 13 and I didn't know his name. My Grandmother Stepp died when I was around 6. Her name was Karen.

At this time, my mother had gotten sick. She went from doctor to doctor, and the doctors couldn't find out what was wrong. Finally, they said she had depression. The doctors sent her to Raleigh, N.C., to receive shock treatment to find out what she was depressed about. The shock treatment would make her forget things about us when we were younger.

When I went to see her in Raleigh, I had just gotten a new haircut and a new dress. She told me how pretty I was. The next day I went back to see her and she did not remember the dress or the haircut. I was so sad to see my mother like that. I was lost without her.

When she came home, she never went anywhere. Her sister, Edith, did all of her shopping for her. I helped out some. My mother met a lady preacher named Mrs. Outlaw. She was good for my mother. She would stop by and pick up my mother to take her out to eat. She also would ride her around and talk to her about God and the need to be saved. Mother had only gone to church for a little while. Daddy took me for a while and would sit out in the car and wait for me.

I met a friend at school. Her name was Faye Williford. She had a sister named Mary Helen and a brother named Jimmy. The Willifords were good to me.

Mrs. Williford was kind to me and sort

of took my mother's place in certain ways. No one could ever completely take her place. She loved us dearly but she was sick and trying to get well. She later would get better and became a wonderful wife and mother. She also became a wonderful Christian lady.

Mrs. Williford would make Faye and me May Day outfits to wear to school. One time, I had warts on both of my hands, and she took broom-straws and pinched each one. She then blindfolded me and took me to the woods, made me dig a hole and put the straw in the hole and cover them back up. The next day, the warts were gone.

Faye and I met another girl in our room at school. Her name was Carolyn Gregory. We three would go out playing and walking all around.

ABOUT THIS time, Mother wanted me to start taking piano lessons. We did not have a piano at home, so at school when we went out to play, I would stay behind and practice on the one at school. I did not like that so I quit. I was no good at it anyway.

My brother started working at a skating rink. Faye and I went there for a while. There were airmen that went there and we would talk to them. Mrs. Williford made us some short skating skirts.

I also got a chance to babysit for the lady that owned the skating rink. The name of it was Goldpark Lake and it was located on the other side of town. I was pretty fair on skates; I could even skate backwards. I worked hard at it. My brother was a wonderful skater. If he had wanted to, he could have gone places with his ability to skate.

There was a lake there and I went a lot even though I couldn't swim. No one ever tried to teach me. My brother was a great swimmer too. He was good at everything he touched. I used to think my mother loved my brother more than me because I wasn't good at anything. She even said he was pretty when he was born and I was not.

By this time I was about fourteen years old. I met a boy named Bobby who wanted me to meet Phil, a boy from nearby Grantham. So I met him, and we would double date with Bobby, the other boy, and his girlfriend some. That was in 1957. Later, Phil and I would date by ourselves. We would go out in a 1957 Chevrolet, the Hood's car.

He took me to church on Sunday nights. He did not curse, smoke or drink. My mother fell in love with him, and so did my grandparents. My mother loved the way he lived. She did not talk about it much, but my daddy drank as we were growing up. He did not let it keep him from working, and he never hit my mother. That is why she loved Phil so much.

She thought that at 14 I had met the man of my dreams. I liked Phil but was not in love with him. I tried to break up with him, and he said he would go over to the river and jump off of the bridge and kill himself. I was only fourteen and thought he would do it, and I didn't want him to do it so I kept on going out with him.

IT WAS the Christmas of 1957 when he offered me an engagement ring and I took it. I was fifteen in January and Phil was not yet eighteen. We married February 15, 1958. I finished the eighth grade and he finished the twelfth.

We did not have to marry. I moved in with his parents at the time. When Phil finished school he joined the Air Force. I stayed there with his parents and kept house for Mrs. Hood while she worked.

Phil had two brothers, Ted and Mark, and one sister, Elaine. Mrs. Hood was so nice to me. She took me to get my picture taken. She made me clothes. She took me in as if I were her daughter.

We went to see Phil when he was out of basic training. We went to Biloxi, Mississippi. The Hoods purchased a trailer for us to live in. Mr. Hood's brother pulled the trailer to Mississippi. We parked it behind the back gate of the Air Force base. The trailer was paid for.

Mrs. Hood sent us nice packages quite often. I was going to have our first child pretty soon. I went in to see the doctor. My first child was in a breach position. I met a neighbor from Tarboro, North Carolina. She was having her baby at the same time as me.

They put me in a room all by myself.

Our daughter was born a few hours later. It was 1958. Her name is Deborah Sue Hood. After I came home, my dad, mother, brother and Aunt Jean came to see us. I was so happy to see them.

Time went on and Phil was being stationed in Great Falls, Montana. His uncle had to pull the trailer back home to North Carolina for a while. The lady I met from Tarboro wanted to ride back with us to North Carolina. There was only room for two in the cab of the truck. So me, her and our babies lay down on the bed in the trailer for the ride home. It was quite an experience.

We parked the trailer back in the Hood's backyard. The Hoods got to see their granddaughter for the first time. When our leave was over, Phil left for Great Falls. I stayed behind for a while.

My daughter and I went on up there a short time later. We took the train; it took two-and-a-half days to get there. It was 2100 miles from home and I was sixteen with an eleven-month-old baby. I had never seen train stations so large.

It was snowing and Phil picked us up in an old Model T Ford. There were holes in the footboard, and you could see the snow on the ground. We stayed on base until our trailer arrived. His uncle pulled it all the way there for us and set it up once he got there, outside the back gate, of course.

IT WAS cold there and snowed from September until April. It got below zero sometimes. We gave out of oil one time, and that was one of the times it got below zero. We almost froze to death. It got so cold that our toilet busted.

People drove in the snow as if it had not snowed at all. You hardly ever saw anyone run off of the road. Soon after that I became pregnant with our second child.

Some of the ladies in the trailer court heard of a nursing course at the hospital so we attended it. We all passed and they put us to work. They liked me there and offered me a job as a ward clerk and I said yes. I took a short course and they put me right on the job. Now days you have to have a high school education or more. I loved it but I had to step away for a while to have the baby.

Our second baby was born on December 8, 1960. His name is William Douglas Hood. I was seventeen then. I went back to work when he was only three weeks old. We had moved on base by then.

We could see the mountains from our house and there was snow on them almost all year. I fell in love with Great Falls. It was a small town.

I went on base to an airmen's meeting where we took a course. I was the youngest ever to attend. They put a picture of us in the newspaper back home in Goldsboro.

Six months after William was born, I got pregnant again. I worked until I was seven months pregnant. Our next son was born on March 4, 1962. Phil dropped me off with the children from the hospital and went to a second job.

Here I was with three children, ages three, one-and-a-half, and two days old. So I fixed all the formula I would need, fixed something to eat, cleaned the house from top to bottom, washed clothes and got everything in line.

That went on for a couple weeks. I woke up in the middle of the night. I was in awful shape. I went to the doctor and he did not know what was wrong with me. He gave me nerve medicine, but I am sure I had postpartum depression. They didn't know what that was then. I would call my mother back home in the middle of the night. I needed her, but she was so far away. I know it hurt her not to be able to help me.

LIFE WENT on. We were in the Air Force almost five years by this time. We got extended for nine months. It was the Cuban Crisis, and we were at a mission base. We got to go home three times, each time with a different amount of time. We drove straight through. He would drive some, then I would drive some. We would pull over on the side of the road an hour or so at the time.

The Hoods came to see us once. They did not know I had been so sick. I was somewhat better then. I did not know much about God then. I had not been to church much, and Phil and I had only been a few times in Great Falls.

I never was able to go back to work. I left Phil before we got out of the service, took the kids and stayed with a friend. Phil wanted to be with the children before he left, so I let him keep the kids for a few days. He would not let me have them back so I got in the car and came back to North Carolina with him. His uncle came and pulled our trailer back to North Carolina later on.

When we got back to North Carolina it was almost Christmas. We went to my granddaddy's Christmas party and some other events. It was the first Christmas with our families in four years. We stayed with the Hoods then.

Phil heard about a two-way radio class in Norfolk, Virginia. So we went up there to see if he could pass the test, and he did. Phil was a very smart man. Then he heard about a job in Kinston, about thirty minutes from where we lived in North Carolina. He went to talk to the man and got the job.

We sold our trailer and bought some furniture and moved to Kinston. Later on I met some girls and an older lady, and they invited me to a dance. So I told Phil I was going somewhere else and went to the dance.

There were lots of Marines there. So I kept going to the dance for some time and met a Marine there. We started going together and I got pregnant. I did not know what to do, so one day I took off back to Goldsboro, back to my parents' house.

Phil came a few days later and wanted us to go home. I would not, so he was trying to put the kids in the car, and we fought. He drove off with my children. That was the worst mistake of my life.

So I went to my parent's lawyer the next day and he told me I could not get my children back if Phil wanted them. I begged him for my baby; he was only one year old. He would not let me have him. So I went out of state and got divorced.

THE MARINE, Don, and I got married.
We cared for each other, but we were not in
love. We moved onto a base called Cherry
Point in Havelock, North Carolina.

I missed my children. Mother and I
would sit and talk about them and cry. See,
when I lost the children, Mother lost her
grandchildren. Debbie, Bill and Greg, you
did not know it, but you were loved.

I was so sad without my children, which was the beginning of my depression. I had pictures of my children in our bedroom. I would lay in bed before I got up and just look at those pictures. I had to move them to another room. I walked everywhere. As the months passed, I went back to my mother's to have the baby.

The baby was a girl, and her name was Gena Marie Madden, born September 10, 1964. My husband came up some time later to see her. He told me he had plans and this messed them up. I said what plans? He said one of his friends just got out of the Marines and they were going to D.C. for the weekend to celebrate. I didn't want to mess up his plans, so he kissed me and left.

That was a happy and sad time for me. No one came to see me. Only the husband and the grandparents were allowed back in the room when you were having a baby. So Don and my daddy came to pick us up after the weekend.

We went back to my parents, so in a few days we went back to Cherry Point. My husband kept going to the dance some without me. He also went with women sexually, he told me. What a mess my life was in.

I moved with my baby back in with my parents. I went to work as a waitress because I had no education. I got a new car and a few other things. Don would come up to my parents and would stay over on the weekends.

Later, we moved back to Cherry Point on base and life went on. Don got sent TDY (Temporary Duty) for six weeks. Gena and I went back to my parents. I worked at the same place I had before.

I saved my money and went back to Cherry Point a few days before he came back. I fixed up the apartment with the money I had made. That did not work out so Gena and I moved back to my parents again, and I went back to work. So he came up to my parents.

On Thanksgiving Day my brother Freeman and Don were driving my car and totaled the car in an accident. Don was not hurt but my brother hurt his back. So I had to wait for another car.

DON SOON got out of the Marines. At this
time, we went to see his parents in Cincin-
nati, Ohio. I wanted to come back home so
we came back to North Carolina.

He wouldn't look for a job. So we
called it quits for the final time. Our
daughter was two and a half. At this time, I
got to see my other children some. I was so
happy to see them.

I was working at a place called the En Cee Cue, a restaurant. It had curbside service, waiting tables, and a cashier's stand. I worked all three at different times.

Later a man came to own the restaurant. He was a little older than I. We started going together. I had to have surgery four times while I worked there.

One of the surgeries that I got was because I got pregnant by the man I was going with. I had my second tubal pregnancy. We dated for four years. He wanted children. I could not have children anymore so we never married.

This business went down so I went to work at Wilbur's BBQ. We kept going together for some time. He went to work at another restaurant. We only saw each other on the weekends. He worked late at night.

I had met a friend while I was working at the En Cee Cue named Linda Massey. She left with me to work at Wilbur's too.

She followed Jimmy one night for me, and he went to an old girlfriend's house.

Jimmy went to work at KFC. Linda and I started going on base to the NCO club. Jimmy and I broke up, and he found someone at his work.

I moved out of my mother's house again. The way I worked was by working split shifts and having Mother keep Gena some. I moved back close to Linda. I met a man named Bill and Linda met a man named John. He became the love of her life.

I broke up with Bill. Linda married John and moved to Rhode Island. Linda came here from England. I moved back in my uncle's trailer next to my parents. I got to see my children once a month; Daddy or I would go and pick them up in Kinston.

IT WAS about this time that I met this lady that came by to my mother's; she was selling something. She said later that she looked at me and knew something was wrong with me. She went to Adamsville Church of God in Goldsboro.

I was in bad shape at this time. I called the lady. Her name was Ann. She and some of the ladies from the church prayed for me. After that, I went to church with her.

I knew I needed God, but did not want to give up the world. They prayed for me a number of times. I was not serious with God, so later they prayed with me. I was possessed with demonic spirits. They had a time with me. The devil wanted me to give up, but I was not going to.

After that, I started going to Bible study. After I got delivered from the demons, cursing spirits would come to my mind and curse, and they would say lots of ugly things to my mind. I never was one for cursing, as it about drove me crazy.

I had all kinds of lust spirits come to me. I even thought of how I could kill myself. I was nervous and depressed. I would go to Ann's often for help. I even called her in the middle of the night. See, the bad spirits were gone out of me and they wanted to enter back into me.

I got so bad I went to Cherry Hospital.

When I was there, they put me in with everyone. Cherry Hospital serves Eastern North Carolina, so they have every kind of people there. I met a woman from out of town and bought her a drink because she had no money. She was a lesbian. I did not know that. She fell in love with me, laid on the hall floor next to my room, and would listen to my phone calls. She even followed me to the bathroom and stood right in front of me while I was on the toilet. She said to me, "Why did you do that to me?" I don't know how, but I got past her.

Later, I got a little better. I went to have a little surgery there. They let me go to the beauty shop to get a perm. So I came home, but I still needed prayer.

I went back to church. The pastor and the people prayed for me and helped me. I was in the church for some time. I met a man named Jimmy through a friend. We dated for a while, and he would go to church with me. He asked me to marry him, so I did. We got married in South Carolina. Lots of people at that time got married there.

AS SOON as we moved in together, he stopped going to church with me. He got drunk a lot and he beat me often. One night he was beating me, and he pushed my head into an iron bedpost and I kind of passed out. As soon as he knew I was all right, he started beating me again.

One time he was beating me, and my daughter Gena got a knife. Luckily, no one was hurt. My son Greg came to live with us but he was either gone to school or out a lot. He was seventeen then and my daughter was 13 at that time.

I had surgery when we were married. He ran out on me often. I worked as a cashier at Ralph's Supermarket. I loved that kind of work. Later, I knew we were not going to stay married so I moved us into a house I could afford.

He got drunk and would lock me out of the house. I had to crawl in the kitchen window sometimes in the morning. One time, he was drunk and my daughter didn't answer the door as soon as he wanted. When she did let him in, he ran her out of the house and down the path at two in the morning. She was seventeen at the time and pregnant.

My son had moved out and had joined the Coast Guard. He worked out of state. He came home on Friday nights. He would give me some money and he would leave. I would not see him anymore for the weekend. I finally convinced him to leave and he moved out for the last time.

Once my oldest daughter came to see me. She ate lunch with me and he had something to say about that.

At this time, my two daughters had babies about a month apart. Debbie had Johnathon and Gena had Jennifer. My two sons had their babies. Bill had Brandon and Greg had Glenn.

Gena and I went to see Greg when his son was born. He was in the Coast Guard at that time in Elizabeth City. Gena and her daughter lived with me. I was still in church and doing fair. Still working. When Jennifer was two weeks old, I went to the bedroom, picked her up out of the crib and got her and myself ready for church.

My brother and his wife got a divorce because he drank a lot. He would take the shirt off his back and give it away to someone who needed it. Penny, his wife, was a very nice lady; they had 3 children together, Carrie, Todd, and the third was a stillborn child. Freeman was still doing body shape work.

THE HOUSE I was living in had high ceilings, and it was hard to heat also. It started mildewing. So I was in a hurry to move. I found a trailer in town and moved in it.

I lost my job about this time. When I got moved in, I saw it was a bad trailer court next to us. I told my mother that it would not do for us to live there in the summer. Gena would lay out in her bikini. I knew that would not work.

This was in January. Gena worked nights and I kept Jennifer. One night my friend and I went to a gospel singing. I came home and prayed before I went to bed. Jennifer had never spent the night off, but she stayed that night at my cousin's, so I went home and went to bed alone. I don't know what woke me up but as soon as I woke up I knew I was not alone. There was a man standing at my bed.

I jumped out of the bed, we fought, and I was out in the hall by then. He told me to stop screaming and to not see him or he would hurt me up good. He had a knife. I felt it.

He cut my clock cord and tied me up. It stopped at 4:45 before daybreak. I did what he asked me to do; he raped me, cut the phone cord, stole my money, and left. Gena was not home yet, so I waited for her.

When she came home, I told her at the door what had happened. She started screaming. So we got ourselves together and called the police and left for the police department.

I called my pastor, my mother, my friend that led me to the Lord, and my cousin that Jennifer was with. So they sent me to the hospital, and from there back to the police. When they got through at the police, my mother had called my two sons and they came up and took me to my mother's. She hugged me when I arrived.

The next day I moved out of that trailer, and moved in with my parents. Daddy and I looked at a used trailer soon after that. He bought it and pulled it onto his lot next door to them. So Gena, Jennifer, and I moved into it.

I got myself together with God's help and spoke at some rape seminars. I went on base to speak. A lady was ahead of me that had been raped. I thought that I had nothing new to say. But I got up and spoke. I thought I made a mess of things. Afterwards a man came up to me and said, "Ma'am, you don't know it but some things you said will save some woman's life here."

I say, if you can get away from your rapist, by all means do that; if not, do as he says and pray he will leave you alone when it is over, like mine did, thank God. I give God all the praise and glory.

Afterwards I would not sleep with my face to the wall like I wanted to, until my daughter came home from work. My friend Ann felt led by God to pray for me that day before I got raped. I am so happy she was led by God and obeyed Him. I could have been killed. Thank God I was not.

I MOSTLY cleaned houses and trailers, and babysat in my home later. I went to church and took people to church. Before seatbelts came in, I had as many as eleven children in my car going to church. Later I drove the van to church, and it was an old van. It had a hole where you would sit on the floor. The heat from the motor would come up to your legs.

You know, when you are saved, you don't get people to go to church that are saved. You reach out to those that are hurting. The demonic, the possessed, anyone you can reach out to.

I was a very nervous person and I got depressed. I think I took after my mother some, plus I was going through the change of life.

I sold plates when we had a dinner, and delivered them all. We also made and sold Easter eggs at Easter. I would go out and get orders and deliver them. We would have a harvest sale and I would look for items to sell. God gave me a talent for that. I could meet people as strangers and start a conversation with them.

The church was good to me. Once Brother Jarman put on some tires for me. More than once the ladies paid my car insurance. Even today at the age of 73, if I really need them and ask them, they have never refused me. And part of the time, I was not going to church there.

One day I was at my trailer. Todd, my brother's son, came over and told me that my brother was found dead at the body shop where he worked. They found him in a car, killed by carbon monoxide. He had killed himself. I only hope at some point he repented. My brother was special to my son, Greg, and he was sad for some time. We all were.

It had been years since I had dated. My daughter had moved out with Jennifer. She lived next to a man named Willis. We started seeing each other and he was much older than me.

We got married later. I knew it was wrong. I would not wait and let God send me someone if it was his will. The same thing happened with Jimmy and look what I went through.

We got married July 5, 1985. The man

was a devil. He was as mean as a rattle-snake. I was scared to death of him.

We lived in my parents' trailer where I had been living, but we argued so he got his own trailer. We could stay together about two weeks, then we separated for two weeks.

He was over at his trailer and he asked me if I would take him to buy groceries when I got home from church. So I said yes and I went over to take him. I knocked on the door and he opened it. He was dog drunk. I went in, which was a mistake, but I wanted my car keys and my house keys. He had been in my trailer when I was not home and picked up some things that were not his.

One time I was so scared of him when I was asleep in my trailer. The back door was closest to my bedroom. I woke up and saw him at my door inside the trailer and he was there to hurt me. He was not actually there but that's just how scared of him I was.

Back at his trailer, we argued. He grabbed me by my dress, tore half the top of my dress off and pushed me down on the couch. I said, "God help me!"

He said, "Don't call on him. He's not going to help you."

He told me to go back to his bedroom. I said to myself, if I wanted help, I'd better holler. I knew I did not holler loud. There were some young people a few trailers over, and they had a bonfire and were out there singing. It was winter and the windows were closed, and in a few minutes they knocked on the door.

He opened it and I went out.

I did not holler that loud; the Holy Ghost took my voice that evening and let those kids hear me, I know that for sure. He is our strength, our helper, and our comforter; he is our everything we need if we let him be.

Then Willis came back to my trailer. Willis and the man next door were drinking and they did not stop at the stop sign. They hit a car and had an accident. The man did not get hurt but Willis did. He was put in the hospital.

WHEN I got home, I called his family from Fayetteville and his sister who lived in Conway, South Carolina. I had met them once before. I told them about his accident. They were not that religious and told me a higher power was looking after me.

They said every woman he was with he had hurt them all. They said he had poured kerosene on his second wife and had tried to burn her to death and still she loved him.

The ex-wife, their children, and one grandson were all nice. They came to see him in the hospital. When I went back to the hospital, I did not act the same. He knew something was wrong. This was on a Sunday.

I went back to work at Wayne Manufacturing as a clothing inspector. My insurance had just come into effect at work. This lady called me from the college. She was studying to be a lawyer. She asked me if she could come see me. She was writing something about a case and she wanted to know if she could take my story about my rape.

I don't know how she found out about me but I said yes. She came that night, the only day I had not gone to the hospital.

As she was leaving, Willis called and said he was hurting in his chest. I told him to tell the nurses. I went on to bed and around 4:00, the hospital called Mother and told her Willis had taken a turn for the worse and to get up there, so Mother and I went.

The doctor and the nurses told us when they made rounds at 3:30 that Willis was dead. I was supposed to bring him home that day. When I got home, I called work and his family. I called my pastor and my friends.

Willis' boss had taken out $10,000 on him in life insurance. At my work I had taken out $2,500 on him. I did not know it, but I was in for the ride of my life.

I made plans for my husband's funeral. We planned on putting him in our family grave plot. I planned on a nice funeral. I spent around $10,000 on the funeral.

His children came to the wake. His grandson wanted to be a pallbearer so I said yes.

MY GOOD friend Paulette and I went out
to eat after church a lot. We went to the
beach one Saturday together. We parked
my car outside one of the busy buildings
that night and slept in the car that night.
When we got up the next morning, we read
our Sunday school lesson and went on to
the beach.

She later died with breast cancer. She

lived cancer free for years. I was with her when the doctor told her. You could hear back in the doctor's office. I was very sad. I called her brothers and sister, and they came to her house that same night. I planned on going to the hospital with her.

I went to see her some when she was having her treatments. I remember putting her in the backseat of my car to go to Kenly Camp Meeting. Her face looked as if she had a bad stroke.

I invited her to take part in my plans for Willis' funeral. I got her to ride in the family car for me. The funeral was nice. After the funeral was over, everyone went back to my trailer to eat and then went home.

I sent pictures of Willis when he was drinking his coffee one morning. I had extras made. I did not put him next to where I would be buried. Maybe that's ugly, but I do not want to lay beside him.

He was mean to me.

His sister told me at the wake that he was not loved as a child. I know that God offers everyone His love and would have given Willis His love if he would have reached out to Him.

A week later, I started having anxiety and depression. I started having anxiety attacks that felt as if I were having a heart attack. I was put in Cherry Hospital but I really did not get any better.

I felt as if I could not handle it anymore. I came home, laid on my couch, and just let my world pass me by. The doctor told Mother that I did not fear that fear anymore that I had since Willis died. That I felt guilty because I was not crying and upset over Willis dying like other widows do.

I was feeling relieved.

I stayed out of church for a long time. I got my insurance money, which they doubled to twenty thousand. The funeral was ten thousand. I spent the rest on everyone else and some on me.

I bought Daddy a lawn mower. I bought Mother a microwave, some clothes, and a Bible. I bought two horses, saddles and bridles, and covers for the saddles. I got a car for five thousand, and two dogs for a thousand. I bought Gena a TV, two phones, a car, and gave her $500.

ABOUT THIS time I started out going back to church. Some of the time I would go, but other times I would have to go back home because of my anxiety.

I went to the emergency room quite a bit. No one knew how I felt but me and God. I would not wish these things on my worst enemy. I was not able to go back to work.

I heard I might could get a VA check. I had a lot of work to do to get it. I knew nothing about Willis' past, past marriages, his service, or where to find any of this out. I really worked hard. I eventually got it, and I started getting $360 a month with a yearly increase.

I was 62 at the time and started drawing social security about the same time. Mother started getting sick and went to the doctor a few times. The doctor phoned the house and I answered. He said they found a large mass on her spine. She spent a few days in the hospital but there was nothing they could do. I brought Mother home with me where I had moved to.

Granddaddy was sick at the time too. Mother died soon after him. I moved a lot after that. I don't know why.

After Mother died Daddy went to the hospital; he mourned the death of my mother. He was depressed and cried a lot. It hurt me badly to see my daddy cry.

He later came home and went on with life. Mother loved my daddy so much. He missed her. My cousin's body shop was next door to Daddy's, and he would help him out. Penny, my brother's wife, was a social worker and she worked hard to help my parents.

Penny and Charles, I want to thank you for all you have done. Penny, you took my place when I was fifteen and went away nearly five years. Mother loved you as if you were her daughter, and you loved her as if you were.

Daddy loved you the same. I used to be a little jealous. I am not anymore. I am grateful for your love of my parents.

Daddy had a heart attack, but he had asked me before, how do you get saved? I told him. I asked him if he had done it, and he said yes. Later Daddy died. I know my mother is happy in heaven.

MY GRANDDAUGHTER came to live with me at the age of twelve. She was hard to handle. She started having babies at the age of fourteen. Little Dustin came along nine months later.

We had some complications with him. The doctor said his head was too large and he possibly could be mentally retarded. He was in the hospital quite some time for spinal meningitis.

I sat with him around the clock. He came home, and I took him to Greenville to see a specialist. He said he was fine, but that he just had a larger head than most babies.

Thank God!

A year and a half later she had Mason. He slept a lot. The doctor said that was okay. Children grow when they sleep a lot.

They were good babies. When they got two I trained them to use the potty in one week. Later Shelly was born, and she was another story entirely. She cried a lot and would not sleep long.

Then Jennifer met a man named Jimmy Dean and they got married. Then Jennifer had another baby, Josh. Jimmy was proud to be a father. He took care of him. Jimmy and Jennifer did drugs a lot. They were so bad that I did not know what to do. I went to church and took the children with me.

They would not work at all. Times were hard. I had to have a knee replacement and could not recover because there was no one to keep house. They only made a mess. We moved a lot.

Jimmy tried to get me to sell drugs in our home. It was tempting, because we needed the money so bad. I was not able to go on. They would not get up to send the kids off to school and cook for them. I did the best I could.

Jennifer heard Social Services was on the way to get the children so took the three oldest to her mother's, and Jimmy took the youngest to his aunt's. I took an outfit and left my belongings, and went to the Salvation Army and stayed until I got my check.

The Salvation Army helped me get a trailer. I babysat some. I moved into a couple more places.

Jennifer had found me. She started

bringing boyfriends with her. They all had prison records and did drugs. She started stealing money from me. I found a senior building that had an apartment for rent. I applied for the apartment there.

I came back later to see where I was on the list. They had an apartment for me. I moved in right away. I did not have much to move in. I was now getting social security. My rent was based on income, and Section Eight paid part of my rent. My rent was $262 for everything. Praise God!

I WAS in heaven but still depressed. I
didn't have a car and couldn't attend
church anymore. Before I moved into my
apartment I went from doctor to doctor. I
was in the hospital a lot. I was so bad that I
could not even shop a lot. I would go up to
be checked out and feel like I was going to
pass out. My psychiatrist helped me work
through that.

People make fun of people that have mental problems. It is a sickness just like a physical sickness. If it had not been for God and the doctors I would have killed myself, I believe. Life was just too heavy for me to bear without God, my friends, and the doctors.

For the first two years I lived here I watched TV a lot, stayed in the apartment a lot, and went to the emergency room with anxiety feeling like I was having a heart attack. No one knows how anxiety makes you feel.

Jennifer was now on the streets for some time. She would come to my apartment, we would go to bed, and she would steal my bank card out of my purse. I would not realize it until she had already been to the bank and gotten the money out. I would give her money also.

I was told to let her go out of my life. I prayed for her and got other people to also.

I was still out of church. I missed my church; I went there twenty-nine years and got saved there.

I was getting sick a lot and found out I had diabetic neuropathy. I had to go to bed sometimes because I could not walk. My blood pressure was high, and also I had a thyroid condition. I weighed 268 pounds. I only had my great-grandchildren and God that made me happy.

So, would you believe that God came on the scene and started turning my life around? I got to go to church some. I was not as depressed. I started getting out some. I started going to Bible study in my building once a week, started fixing up my apartment, and started having an aide to help me.

Jennifer was still around on payday. She even took so much of my money one time that I had to get the manager to take me to my friend's to borrow some money so I could pay my rent. Jennifer has seen her friends get killed. She has been stabbed really bad. I felt if I let her go, that was all the family I had left.

A FEW years ago I asked the Lord, "What can I do for you? I have no car to go anywhere." The Lord spoke to my heart and said to me, "There are 41 apartments here that you can minister to."

That's what I started doing. I have given out Get Well Soon cards, and I pray with them if they ask me to. See, the people here are elderly like me and some have sickness often.

I also go to Bible study often. The ladies from across the road come over for Bible study, and they lead our Bible study, too. They always come on the fourth Wednesday of the month. They fix us dinner and we discuss different things. They are from the Greenleaf Christian Church Disciples of Christ. They give us Thanksgiving parties and other parties for other holidays.

Mrs. Stella asked us to take over the Christmas party. My neighbor Doretha does the bingo, so I took over the rest. To my amazement, I was able to do it. I get up from the start of the party to the end. This past Christmas was my third year directing the party.

One morning I got up and sat in my recliner to say a simple prayer. I asked God to help me to lose weight. I told him I wanted to feel better and look better. That's all I said.

God helped take my appetite from me, and from October of 2014 to February of 2015, I lost almost a hundred pounds. I felt better and looked better. My doctor was amazed and wanted to know what I was doing. The only thing was that he would not take me off the drug that hurt my kidneys.

He did not tell me my kidneys were getting bad. So I went to a new doctor. The first time I went to him, he checked me and told me if I took any more of that medicine for diabetes I would be a very sick woman. I was no longer a diabetic.

He took blood work the next time. I had an appointment but he called me back in before my appointment. My kidneys were not working like they should. They were only working at one-third capacity.

I am currently going to a kidney doctor to see how things work out. My blood pressure is down, and my feet hardly hurt anymore.

MY GREAT-grandsons came over for Thanksgiving and Christmas for a big meal. I cooked all by myself and cleaned up all by myself. I am in charge of Bible study with Mrs. Patterson helping me. I am reading throughout the week to make sure I have a few things to say. I don't know what God will do next!

I finally told Jennifer to go and leave

me alone until she could learn to think of others and take care of her own finances. I love her dearly and I still believe that she will turn her life around. God uses the lowest of sinners sometimes. Look what she could do on the streets to help people she knows. She has been on the streets for 15 years now.

I pray all the time for my children and grandchildren to get saved. They will never know the depression that I have had wanting them dearly in my life. I love them dearly but I have finally moved on with my life, thanks to God.

I can never thank God enough for his love for me. God has grown my ministry. I go to the local Senior Center twice a week and let them know of God's Word. I encourage them and let them know that if they let God in their life, God can do wonders and he has a home for them in heaven.

Also I want to thank so many people who have helped me along my journey. My dear friend that led me to the Lord, Ann. My dear friend Rhonda McDuffie, who is a minister. Most of all, I am thankful for God and the Holy Spirit.

I am happy. I finally found peace in God. God loves me (and you) so much. He put up with my faults until I changed my life around. He saw not what I was, but what I could become. Praise God. I love the Lord and want him to be first in my life.

God has helped me change my life around completely. I lost weight, I no longer hurt in my feet, and I no longer walk with a walker or cane. I no longer have diabetes. I walk a lot with my little dog, Daisy. I exercise at the Senior Center a lot. I am a new woman.

People would never believe what I have been through. I am so happy. God has made a different woman out of me.

If God can do all of that for me, he can help any of you who might read this. If you take the first step, he will move mountains for you. He is the love of my life.

Thanks to God and everyone who has prayed for me and lifted me up in ways I never imagined possible.

About the Author

Linda doesn't pretend to be a preacher. She simply feels called to minister to people. She has a compulsion to show God's gracious love, His tender mercy, and His eternal salvation to everyone she meets.

Over the years, she has worked a number of jobs, among her favorites being a cashier at Brookside Open Air Market and Ralph's Supermarket. She loves to count money – other people's money, especially! Linda is looking forward to the birth of her first great-great-grandchild, a girl, by Dustin and Christina, due September 8, 2016. Her name will be Damilia.

Linda has many grandchildren. She would like to see the ones she has never met and hold them all dear to her heart. Now retired, she enjoys attending the Senior Center in her hometown of Goldsboro, North Carolina, where she currently resides.

Three years ago, at a low point in her life, she cried out to God, asking Him what she could do to share His gospel with others. She found her answer amid the residents of the apartment building she calls home.

Linda took on God's challenge, and she hasn't slowed down since.